I Bet You Didn't Know That ...

FISH SLEEP WITH THEIR EYES OPEN

and Other Facts and Curiosities

FISH SLEEP WITH THEIR EYES OPEN

and Other Facts and Curiosities

by Carol Iverson • pictures by Jack Lindstrom

 Lerner Publications Company • Minneapolis

With thanks to Gary DeGrote and his sixth graders,
Addi Engen, Isabel Marvin, Joan Ennis, Torild
Homstad, and my husband, Art

Copyright © 1990 by Lerner Publications Company

Library of Congress Cataloging-in-Publication Data

Iverson, Carol.
  Fish sleep with their eyes open and other facts and curiosities /
Carol Iverson; pictures by Jack Lindstrom
      p.   cm. – (I bet you didn't know that)
  Summary: Presents a variety of miscellaneous facts about fish,
birds, insects, and other animals.
    ISBN 0-8225-2277-2 (lib. bdg.)
    1. Animals – Miscellanea – Juvenile literature. [1. Animals –
Miscellanea. 2. Curiosities and wonders.] I. Lindstrom, Jack, ill.
II. Title. III. Series: Iverson, Carol. I bet you didn't know that.
QL49.I93   1990
591 – dc20   89-27184
                                                              CIP
                                                               AC

Manufactured in the United States of America

1 2 3 4 5 6 7 8 9 10 99 98 97 96 95 94 93 92 91 90

I Bet You Didn't Know That...

The ostrich cannot fly, but it can run as fast as
40 miles an hour (64 kilometers per hour).

I Bet You Didn't Know That...

The bald eagle is not really bald. The bird's head is covered with white feathers and from far away it looks bald.

Baby ducks are born knowing how to swim.

A young robin eats more than its weight in earthworms every day.

Shellac is made from a sticky substance given off by insects.

There are more than 800,000 different kinds of insects.

I Bet You Didn't Know That...

Some tropical catfish swim upside down while they eat.

Seen from the front, the hatchet fish looks almost as thin as a sheet of paper.

Because of the size of its mouth and its ability to expand its stomach, the angler fish can swallow other fish that are larger than itself.

The seahorse is the only fish that swims upright.

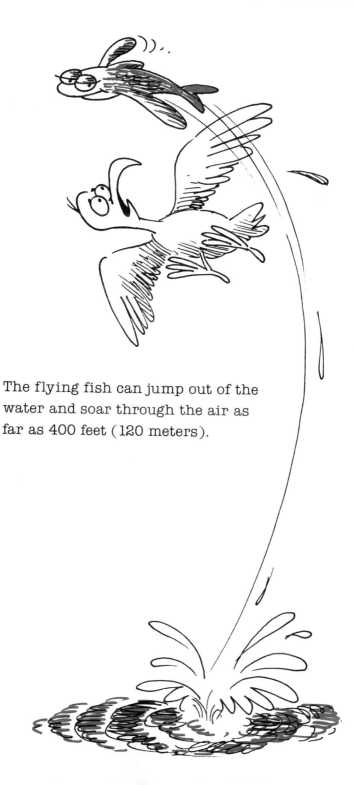

The flying fish can jump out of the water and soar through the air as far as 400 feet (120 meters).

I Bet You Didn't Know That...

The smallest bird is the hummingbird. Some hummingbirds are only two inches (5 centimeters) long.

Birds cannot move their eyeballs. They must turn their entire heads to look around.

A bird's eyes often weigh more than its brain.

Some birds have special locking
mechanisms in their feet that
prevent the birds from falling off
their perches while they sleep.

I Bet You Didn't Know That...

There are more than 8,000 different kinds
of ants.

An ant can lift an object 52 times its own weight.
This is like a person being able to lift four tons.

Working alone, a bee would
have to make 60,000 trips of
about one and one-half miles
(2.4 km) each to make one
pound (.45 kilograms)
of honey.

Bumblebees make their nests in grass or in
shallow holes in the ground.

When a fly walks, little pads on its feet secrete
a sticky liquid that holds the fly to slippery
surfaces.

Only female mosquitoes bite.

I Bet You Didn't Know That...

The kiwi is the only bird that has nostrils at the tip of its bill.

Not all swans are white. One Australian species is almost completely black.

The mockingbird
can meow like a cat
and bark like a dog.

RUFF! RUFF RUFF

Many birds, including chickens, have one eye on each side of their heads. Each eye sees a different scene.

Blue jays bury nuts so they will have food to eat during the winter.

I Bet You Didn't Know That...

An albatross can drink sea water because it has special glands above its eyes that remove excess salt from its body.

An owl can turn its head around to look at things that are directly behind it.

Birds lose all their feathers at least once a year.

Some butterflies
migrate thousands
of miles during the
winter, just like
many birds.

One African beetle survives in the rainless
desert by drinking fog.

Most insects do not have ears. They feel sound
waves and other vibrations with their antennae.

I Bet You Didn't Know That...

A cricket's ears are on its front legs.

Only the male cricket can chirp.

The dragonfly has six legs, but it cannot walk.

A flea can jump 13 inches (32.5 cm) – 130 times its own height. If a person would do that, he or she could jump over the Eiffel Tower.

A fly can beat its wings 12,000 times a minute.

The housefly has more than 4,000 lenses in each eye.

A centipede can have as many as 177 pairs of legs.

I Bet You Didn't Know That...

The piranha, a fish that lives in the Amazon River and is feared by humans and other animals, is usually less than two feet (.6 m) long.

The world's largest frog is the Goliath frog of West Africa. It can weigh up to seven pounds (3 kg) and can measure 14 inches (35 cm) from head to tail. With its legs stretched out, the frog can be almost three feet (1 m) long.

The purse crab of the Pacific and Indian oceans often climbs palm trees to eat young coconuts.

The climbing birds called
nuthatches can walk down
a tree headfirst.

I Bet You Didn't Know That...

The age of many fish can be determined by counting the rings on their scales.

The beluga sturgeon is the largest freshwater fish in the world. It can weigh as much as 3,000 pounds (1,350 kg).

Swordfish can swim faster than a mile a minute
(96 km/h).

Minnows have teeth in their throat instead of
in their jaws.

South Sea islanders once used inflated por-
cupine fish as war helmets.

I Bet You Didn't Know That...

The house crow of Asia seems to be able to live only in cities.

The largest bird is the ostrich. It can weigh up to 200 pounds (90 kg) and grow to be eight feet (240 cm) tall.

The cry of the whooping crane can be heard several miles away.

A woodpecker can peck more than 70,000 times an hour.

The bee hummingbird of Cuba lays its eggs in a nest the size of a walnut shell.

I Bet You Didn't Know That...

The sooty albatross sometimes travels over 200 miles (320 km) in a day.

An albatross can stay in the air for several days, often without flapping its wings for long periods as it glides.

Racing pigeons, flying with a tail wind, have been clocked at speeds of up to 70 miles an hour (112 km/h).

I Bet You Didn't Know That...

Some adult flatfish, including flounders, have both eyes on the same side of their heads.

Many fish have taste buds over much of their bodies.

The skin of sharks is so rough that it can be used like sandpaper.

A whale is not a fish. It is a mammal.

The flamingo lays its egg on top of a nest that is made of mud and looks like a miniature volcano.

The extinct elephant bird's egg was so large that it could have held about 148 hen's eggs.

I Bet You Didn't Know That...

The power of an electric eel could light ten 100-watt light bulbs.

As it swims, the lantern fish creates its own light.

A fish never stops growing.

Fish sleep with their eyes open. They have no eyelids, so they cannot close their eyes.

About the Author
Carol Iverson has been collecting interesting facts and trivia for the **I Bet You Didn't Know That** books for many years. Formerly a dental assistant, Iverson now spends much of her time writing for children. She lives in Northfield, Minnesota, with her husband, Art.

About the Artist
Artist **Jack Lindstrom** is a native of Minneapolis and a partner in a Minneapolis art studio. Lindstrom graduated from the Minneapolis College of Art and Design and currently illustrates a syndicated comic strip for United Features.